DISCARD

HOTDRINKS

HOTDRINKS

Cider, Coffee, Tea, Hot Chocolate, Spiced Punch, Spirits

Mary Lou Heiss and Robert J. Heiss

PHOTOGRAPHY BY MARSHALL GORDON

TEN SPEED PRESS
Berkeley | Toronto

Ten Speed Press
PO Box 7123
Berkeley, California 94707
www.tenspeed.com

Distributed in Australia by Simon and Schuster Australia, in Canada by Ten Speed Press Canada, in New Zealand by Southern Publishers Group, in South Africa by Real Books, and in the United Kingdom and Europe by Publishers Group UK.

Text design by Kate Basart
Food styling by Kim Konecny
Prop styling by Julia Scahill
Photography assistance by Nicki Loverso and Robin Johnson

Library of Congress Cataloging-in-Publication Data
Heiss, Mary Lou.
   Hot drinks : cider, coffee, tea, hot chocolate, spiced punch, spirits /
Mary Lou Heiss and Robert J. Heiss.
      p. cm.
Summary: "A collection of fifty alcoholic and nonalcoholic hot drink
recipes suitable for cold-weather and holiday entertaining, featuring more
than thirty full-color photographs"
   Includes index.
   ISBN 978-1-58008-884-8
   1. Beverages. I. Heiss, Robert J. II. Title.
   TX815.H44 2007
   641.2—dc22   2007016977

Printed in China
First printing, 2007
1 2 3 4 5 6 7 8 9 10 — 11 10 09 08 07

contents

introduction

When the long days of summer turn cool and crisp, we stow away outdoor grills and retreat to the warmth of the kitchen. After we replenish the pantry and sift through our favorite cold-weather recipes, comforting oven-baked dishes make a reappearance on the dinner table. And as fall colors fade into winter, each month brings new opportunities to gather family and friends together in celebration of the coming holiday season.

As our menus change with the season, our preferences in beverages also shift, from icy warm-weather refreshers to enticing cold-weather warmers. *Hot drinks*— the very words conjure sensations of coziness, comfort, and a kaleidoscope of sweet, spicy, and creamy goodness. With a wealth of flavors and a wide variety of inviting tastes, the palette of hot drinks offers something for everyone: smooth chocolates, tantalizing coffees, cosmopolitan teas and tisanes, fruited punches, bedtime soothers, and stylish cocktails.

Whether familiar or exotic, sweet or savory, hot drinks have a magical aura. Regardless of whether they include alcohol, hot drinks express hospitality and conviviality on any occasion: a casual luncheon, a formal soiree, a board game in front of a crackling fire, or a family gathering to celebrate a special moment. It seems like only seconds until the toasty glow from a hot beverage warms us from head to toe.

So dust off your punch bowl, set out your finest cups and saucers, or wrap your chilly hands around your favorite oversized mug. Treat yourself—and your loved ones or guests—to the pleasures of the easy-to-prepare and dressed-up drinks in this book. In these pages, you'll find the perfect beverage for every phase of autumn and winter.

Hot glasses of Moroccan Mint Tea (page 28), made with fistfuls of fresh mint plucked from the late-season garden, allow us to connect with the fading warmth of summer for one last moment.

After an afternoon of cheering on the hometown football team, treat the gang to steaming mugs of Mayan Hot Chocolate with Chile and Orange (page 5) or the appropriately named Bonfire (page 22).

When the family gathers around the table for a pumpkin carving contest, serve a platter of homemade cookies accompanied by tall glasses of Hot Milk Chocolate and Vanilla Ice Cream Soda (page 10) or Spicy Mulled Cider (page 27).

Whether you're the veteran host of the annual Thanksgiving gathering or a new-lywed hosting the family gathering for the first time, surprise your guests with a pitcher of Hot Wasabi Red Snappers (page 44) or start a new tradition by serving an appetite-whetting round of Admiral's Rum and Brandy Punch (page 60) or West Indies Pineapple Cups (page 62). And for the perfect postprandial treat to celebrate a fabulous meal, present an elegant tray of demitasse cups filled with rich Café Vien-noise (page 7) or Café Brûlot (page 8).

When the north wind scatters the last leaves of autumn, bare-branched silhou-ettes remind us that the blustery days of winter—and the festive holiday season—are approaching. This yuletide, chase away the bah-humbug blues by rounding up friends and family to celebrate in gatherings large or small. A glittery punch bowl filled with ruby red Cranberry Claret Cup (page 75) or a traditional Wassail (page 65) brings holi-day cheer and classy sophistication to wintry social events. And what cold-weather activity is complete without a spirited recap over rich cups of Hot Speculatius (page 86) around the kitchen table?

De-stress after a flurry-filled day of holiday shopping and gift wrapping with a soothing mug of Snowflake Vanilla White Chocolate (page 14) or snuggle up with a loved one and share a seductive Angel's Kiss (page 76).

A unique or unexpected drink can turn any occasion into a festive one, so savvy hosts serve signature drinks when they want to turn things up a notch. Increase the wow factor at your next winter party by offering sleek glasses of Fire and Ice (page 55) or toasting cups of Mistletoe and Holly (page 50).

Whether you're partial to the Monk's Robe (page 33), a grown-up variation of a childhood favorite, or the piquant and peppery Masala Chai (page 32), you're sure to find more than a few new favorites in this book. Any of these recipes can be adjusted to suit your taste. Use them as templates for experimentation to create your own repertoire of hot drinks.

And when you ring in the New Year with Pan-Asian Pear William (page 54) cock-tails, you might just end up being the toast of the town. Cheers!

pantry essentials

If you keep a few key pantry ingredients on hand, you'll be ready to whip up a batch of tasty hot drinks whenever the occasion arises. Nearly all of the ingredients in these recipes are readily available, and acceptable substitutions are suggested for more unusual items. Some liquors can be purchased in small amounts, which means you can amass a collection of new tastes without spending a fortune.

absolut citron and absolut peppar

The Swedish company Absolut is known for its flavored vodkas that incorporate all-natural ingredients ranging from chile peppers to vanilla to citrus and other fruits. Absolute Citron is flavored with lemon and lime, and Absolut Peppar is flavored with red and green chile peppers and a suspected dash of ground chile.

apple cider

Depending on where you live, you may be able to purchase sweet apple cider year-round. Look for cloudy, fresh-pressed cider made by an orchard or cider maker in your area. Avoid using crystal clear apple juice, which lacks the full flavor and body of freshly pressed cider.

aquavit

Also known as *akvavit*, this crystal-clear spirit is the national drink of several Scandinavian countries. *Aquavit*, which means "water of life," is intended to be drunk ice-cold and plain with food. Although it closely resembles vodka, it has a refreshing light caraway flavor that makes it a good choice for adding subtle flavor when crafting cocktails.

blood orange bitters

All varieties of bitters are used as an accent flavoring and to give desirable astringency and pull (a term used to describe dryness) to well-made cocktails and mixed drinks. Bitters can be used to stimulate appetites before a meal or to help with overindulgence afterward. Most formulas are a proprietary blend of ingredients and may include herbs, berries, fruits, roots, and flowers. Some bitters contain alcohol, others do not. If you can't find blood orange bitters, orange bitters can be used in its place.

cardamom

Cardamom, a member of the ginger family, is native to India and Sri Lanka. Its seed-pods, used for culinary purposes, are available in white and green varieties. White cardamom is green cardamom that has been bleached with sulfur dioxide to sweeten the flavor and round out the aroma. White cardamom is commonly used in Scandinavian and German baked goods. Green cardamom is used throughout India, Indonesia, and Sri Lanka to flavor meat and vegetable curries and in aromatic spice blends. For the best flavor, crack each pod open with your fingertips or a mortar and pestle. While the pods add visual interest, it is the aromatic black seeds within the pods that contain the flavor.

ceylon cinnamon sticks

Ceylon cinnamon is one of the two species of cinnamon cultivated in Sri Lanka and Indonesia. Ceylon cinnamon sticks, found in specialty food stores, are easily recognized due to their distinctive appearance. Look for brittle, flaky light brown quills that are tightly wound like a rolled paper document and have a fine, sweet aroma. Feel free to substitute hard cinnamon sticks (which are really cassia, the fragrant bark of an evergreen tree related to but different from true cinnamon) if you cannot find soft Ceylon cinnamon sticks.

chambord

This wildly popular cognac-based French liqueur, which has been made in the Loire Valley since the late 1600s, is generously flavored with raspberries and blackberries and tempered with Madagascar vanilla, citrus peel, and honey. It's easy to recognize in its distinctive bottle resembling a crown.

chiles

Volumes can (and have) been written about the immense variety of chile peppers and their wide range of flavors and hotness ratings. For an unusual twist on hot chocolate, experiment with adding a bit of ground ancho, Chimayo, or pasilla chiles; these varieties rank about 5 on a hotness scale of 1 to 10. They impart wonderful chile flavor, as well as moderate heat, and are nicely complemented by sweet spices such as cinnamon, ginger, clove, and nutmeg.

citrus twists

To make citrus twists, use a handheld citrus zester, commonly known as a channel knife, to peel long strips of zest from oranges, lemons, limes, and other citrus fruits. A twist adds a wonderfully intense hit of fresh citrus flavor to cocktails, punch, hot tea, and espresso. The zest contains concentrated citrus oils and its flavor is quite different from the citrus flesh. Don't chisel too deeply into the rind; the white pith beneath the rind is bitter.

cocoa powder

A natural product of chocolate manufacture, dry cocoa powder is obtained when natural cacao butter is removed from cacao nibs. Dutch process cocoa is treated with an alkali to reduce the natural bitterness of the cocoa and give it a richer, darker flavor. Look for the following brands: Bensdorp, Droste, Van Houten, Michel Cluizel, Slitti, and Valrhona.

coffee

When making specialty coffee drinks, use the freshest coffee beans possible and brew the coffee strong. It's best to use Viennese or French roast, or another dark roast, and brew the coffee in a French press or an espresso pot. Both of these methods will allow some soluble solids to remain in the brew, so that the coffee has a desirable level of cloudiness.

cream

While cream hardly needs a definition, the various types of cream available can be confusing. Light cream must contain between 18 and 30 percent milk fat, whipping cream must contain between 30 and 36 percent milk fat, and heavy cream must contain at least 36 percent milk fat. Only whipping cream and heavy cream have a high enough fat content to maintain stable peaks when whipped. The firmness of whipped cream is determined by the length of time it's whipped. Some drinks require a dollop of firmly whipped heavy cream as it holds its shape best. Other drinks require lightly whipped cream, which gives a loose texture that must be spooned over the top of the drink.

drambuie

This Scottish liqueur, based on a blend of aged Scotch whiskies and sweetened with honey, is made from a secret recipe that has been closely guarded by the MacKinnon family for more than 250 years. Reported to be the personal drink of rebel Prince Charles Edward Stuart, Drambuie is rumored to contain saffron and nutmeg among its ingredients. The name *Drambuie* is based on the Gaelic phrase "An Dram Buidheach," which means "the drink that satisfies."

dulce de leche

Dulce de leche is a caramel-like milk-based spread that is popular throughout Latin America. Because of its creamy texture, it can be lavished on muffins or bread right from the jar, heated and used as an ice cream topping, or spooned into hot drinks to add rich, slightly caramelized sweetness.

fleur de sel

The name of this artisanal French sea salt means the "flower of salt." Strictly top-shelf, it's made from pure seawater off the coast of Brittany in northwest France. Although *fleur de sel* is expensive, it provides a wonderful counterbalance to the sweetness of caramel, chocolate, or cream, and usually only a small amount is needed.

frangelico

This fragrant, luxurious Italian liqueur is made from roasted wild hazelnuts from the Piedmont region of northern Italy, in the foothills of the Alps. Reportedly first made 300 years ago by its namesake Fra Angelico, a hermit, this liqueur is made from a traditional recipe that features cocoa, vanilla, and forest berries among its roster of natural ingredients.

hpnotiq

This ultrachic sky blue French liqueur is made from a blend of premium vodka, natural tropical fruit juices, and a touch of cognac. In addition to bringing a warm touch of the Caribbean to any party, it infuses cocktails with an intoxicating blue color.

junmai ginjo sake

The national drink of Japan, sake is made from special varieties of short-grain rice that are polished to varying degrees and fermented with pure water. While a dizzying array of sakes are available in specialty wine shops, look for a fruity and fragrant sake in the *junmai ginjo* style for use in hot drinks.

limoncello

A product of Naples and the island of Capri, this famous Italian aperitif is made from clear, flavorless spirits, water, sugar, and the outermost peel of locally grown Sorrento lemons. Limoncello is usually served straight up in small glasses from a bottle kept on ice in the freezer.

madeira

One of the great fortified wines of the world, Madeira hails from its namesake island, located off the southern coast of Portugal. Like port, it gains substance and heft from fortification, the addition of brandy to the wine either before or after fermentation. In part due to their full, robust flavors, fortified wines have been used for centuries in libations such as punch and wassail.

matcha

Matcha is the powdered green tea used in the Japanese tea ceremony. Because of its dark emerald color, it's also used to lend a vivid hue to beverages and baked goods made with green tea. *Matcha*'s dry and somewhat astringent flavor combines deliciously with sweet flavors.

midori

This proprietary melon liqueur was created by Suntory in Japan in the 1980s. Midori has a stunning emerald color and a heady aroma of perfectly ripe honeydew melon.

mint

You can most likely find fresh mint year-round at the grocer's or your local Asian market. The wrinkly leafed variety is a wonderful herb to experiment with during the dark months of winter. The exhuberant aroma and flavor of fresh mint brings a welcome bit of summer freshness into the winter kitchen. It can be added to either black or green tea and is used to make minted hot chocolate as well.

sherry pepper sauce

A product of Bermuda and Jamaica, this versatile sauce is made from a mixture of spices and hot chiles that have been mascerated in sherry. Thin and clear, it adds bone-dry, crisp heat to drinks and other recipes. Do not substitute hot sauces made with tomatoes or fruit.

star anise

One of the most aromatic of the sweet spices, star anise is most widely cultivated in China, India, and Vietnam. The star-shaped pods flaunt eight perfect points, each of which contains a shiny little seed. In commerce, star anise pods are often broken, but don't worry—just use eight individual points to make one whole star anise.

sugar

The best sugars are made from sugarcane and are unrefined. The process of extracting and then evaporating the juice from sugarcane results in flavorful sugars with varying amounts of natural molasses still present. The more molasses, the darker and stickier the sugar will be. Highly refined white sugar, which has virtually no flavor, just sweetness, has had all of the natural cane molasses removed. In recipes that call for sugar and don't specify type, we recommend granulated sugar.

Demerara sugar is a large-grained, semidry raw sugar with enough molasses content to add a tint of color and a slightly caramelized brown sugar flavor. Turbinado sugar or evaporated cane juice (both raw sugar, as well) or light brown sugar can be used as a substitute, but do not substitute muscovado or dark brown sugar.

European-style sugar cubes are available in white or brown sugar. These irregularly shaped, somewhat lumpy sugar cubes have a rough texture and a grainy surface. They are different from standard sugar cubes, which have a smooth finish and have been cut into even cubes.

Superfine sugar, also known as bar sugar, is often preferable for use in beverages because, as the name implies, it's very finely granulated, allowing it to dissolve almost instantly in cold liquids. When dissolving sugar into hot liquids, it isn't as important to use superfine sugar.

sugar syrups

Flavored sugar syrups in a rainbow of colors and flavors are used in cafés to add a combination of flavors to coffee and tea drinks. You can do the same at home with a well-chosen selection of flavors that you like. Look for brands, such as Monin, that use natural ingredients.

sweet lemonade

Making lemonade from scratch is ideal, but frozen lemonade concentrate is the next best thing. To give frozen concentrate a fresher flavor, add some freshly squeezed lemon juice and use less water than is called for.

tea

True tea contains caffeine and is made from the leaves of the *Camellia sinensis* bush and manufactured into six major classes—green, yellow, white, oolong, black, and pu-erh. These teas yield different tasting brews. Most spiced tea recipes call for strong black tea; look for loose-leaf tea or tea bags from Kenya or the Assam region of India. When choosing a green tea, be aware that Chinese and Japanese green teas have different flavor profiles. When Chinese green tea is called for, purchase tea from a specialty tea shop or look for Stash Premium Green Tea teabags available nationwide. For recipes using Japanese green tea, use Stash Sushi Bar Mild Green Tea teabags or Peet's Sencha teabags.

chapter 1
chocolatesandcoffees

parisafterdark

Undecided about whether to serve coffee or hot chocolate? This gloriously rich drink doesn't force you to choose. Inspired by savvy Parisians, who enjoy their after-dinner coffee with small pieces of dark chocolate, this sophisticated, continental-style brew combines both beloved flavors. The topping of whipped cream sprinkled with a pinch of *fleur de sel* (French sea salt) adds a contemporary twist.

Serves 2

4 teaspoons sugar
4 teaspoons Dutch process cocoa powder
4 teaspoons heavy cream
1½ cups strong, freshly brewed coffee
¼ cup heavy cream, firmly whipped with 1 teaspoon sugar, for garnish
Pinch of fleur de sel for garnish

- In each of two mugs, mix 2 teaspoons of the sugar and 2 teaspoons of the cocoa until well-blended and lump free. Add 2 teaspoons of the cream to each and stir until thoroughly combined into a light paste. Add ¾ cup of the coffee to each and stir again until thoroughly mixed.

- Top each with a dollop of whipped cream. Roll the dollop over to stain it with the coffee, then sprinkle a few grains of fleur de sel atop the whipped cream.

mayanhotchocolatewith chileandorange

As early as 600 BCE, Mesoamericans living in Mexico and Central and South America drank a thick, strong beverage made from roasted cacao to which they added chiles, honey, flowers, nuts, or vanilla. This recipe is a nod to that tradition, combining chocolate, chile, and orange to create a flavorful hot cocoa with a piquant chile bite.

Serves 2

1 ounce bittersweet chocolate (72% cacao), coarsely chopped
4 teaspoons Dutch process cocoa powder
4 teaspoons sugar
½ teaspoon ground ancho or Chimayo chiles
¼ teaspoon ground cinnamon
4 teaspoons heavy cream
1½ cups water
4 orange wedges
2 Ceylon cinnamon sticks for garnish

- Melt the chocolate in a 4-cup glass measuring cup in a microwave for 90 seconds at 70 percent power.

- Combine the cocoa powder, sugar, chiles, and cinnamon in a small bowl. Blend together until thoroughly combined and lump free. Add the cream and stir well to make a thick paste.

► continued on page 6

- Add the paste to the melted chocolate, mix well, then add the water and stir until thoroughly combined. Heat in the microwave for 90 seconds at 70 percent power, stirring once after 45 seconds.

- Serve in two Mexican pottery mugs. Squeeze 1 orange wedge into each, divide the hot chocolate evenly between the mugs, and stir well. Garnish with the remaining orange wedges and the cinnamon sticks.

caféviennoise

The gilded city of Vienna is famous for rich, full-bodied coffee, irresistible chocolate pastries, and the Vienna Mozart Orchestra. Raise a glass of this luscious beverage in honor of all three and let the heady aroma take you on a virtual vacation. Though many brands of chocolate liqueur are available, we're sure the maestro would approve of his namesake Mozart chocolate liqueur, produced in Salzburg, his birthplace.

Serves 4

2 tablespoons (1 ounce) white crème de cacao

2 tablespoons (1 ounce) coffee liqueur

¼ cup (2 ounces) Mozart chocolate liqueur

1½ cups strong, freshly brewed coffee

¼ cup heavy cream, firmly whipped with 1 teaspoon sugar, for garnish

- Blend the crème de cacao and coffee liqueur together in a small measuring cup or pitcher.

- Add the chocolate liqueur to the hot coffee and divide it evenly among four demitasse cups. Top each with a dollop of whipped cream and drizzle 1 tablespoon of the mixed liqueurs over the cream in each cup.

cafébrûlot

This is a slight revamp of a classic recipe published in the 1960s by the now-defunct Pan-American Coffee Bureau in New York. Though the original recipe calls for flambéing in a chafing dish by candlelight in a darkened room, it's okay to forgo the spectacle and make Café Brûlot in your kitchen. Burn off the alcohol completely when you flambé to give the drink a lush, full flavor. No matter where you prepare it, this spirited coffee drink always steals the show.

Serves 4

½ cup (4 ounces) cognac or brandy
2 5-inch Ceylon cinnamon sticks
8 whole cloves
6 European-style sugar cubes
1 ounce semisweet or bittersweet chocolate (55 to 70% cacao),
    coarsely chopped
2 orange twists (see page xi)
2 lemon twists (see page xi)
1½ cups double-strength, freshly brewed coffee

- Combine the cognac, cinnamon sticks, cloves, sugar cubes, chocolate, and citrus twists in a chafing dish or saucepan over very low heat. Do not stir. When the chocolate starts to melt, ignite the cognac with a match. As the cognac burns off, stir with a flameproof spoon to melt the chocolate and dissolve the sugar. After 1 to 2 minutes, or when the flame extinguishes itself, add the hot coffee and stir until thoroughly combined.

- Ladle or strain into demitasse cups and serve hot.

caféconleche

A close relative of cappuccino and café au lait, café con leche is one of the classic coffee drinks. Whereas a cappuccino is a double espresso combined with an equal amount of steamed milk and a café au lait is equal parts scalded milk and strong coffee (not espresso), a café con leche combines two parts hot frothed milk to one part espresso. The milk is usually steamed, not scalded, and the coffee is traditionally a single espresso, but quantities may vary.

Even coffee lovers who like it black have been known to fall under the spell of a properly made café con leche. The secret is in the coffee—it must be freshly roasted and ground right before using. Select coffee that is dark and rich, such as the aromatic and full-bodied coffees from Central and South America, and never use instant coffee. Leave the cinnamon in the spice cabinet—no self-respecting café con leche has cinnamon on top.

Serves 4

1 cup freshly brewed espresso
2 cups whole milk, heated and frothed

- Serve in traditional-size teacups with saucers. Pour ¼ cup of espresso and ½ cup frothed milk into each of four cups and serve hot.

Note: If you have an espresso machine that steams milk, this recipe is simple. If not, you'll need a stove-top espresso maker, a battery-operated or pump-style milk frother, and a saucepan for heating the milk. If you use an espresso machine, whole or 2 percent milk will froth well. When using a handheld frother, whole milk works best. Never use 1 percent or skim milk, however, as neither has the proper amount of milk solids to form a good foam.

hotmilkchocolateandvanilla icecreamsoda

This recipe was designed for sherry or port glasses, so the finished quantity is small. For extra creaminess, use milk chocolate instead of chocolate syrup. If you can't find Demerara sugar, use another variety of raw sugar or light brown sugar to rim the glasses.

Serves 4

2 tablespoons Dutch process cocoa powder for rimming
2 tablespoons Demerara sugar for rimming
½ cup whole milk
1 ounce milk chocolate, coarsely chopped
½ cup seltzer
½ cup premium vanilla ice cream
8 maraschino cherries for garnish

- Blend the cocoa powder and sugar together on a small plate. Run a wet finger around the rim of each glass and quickly press the rim into the cocoa mixture. Shake off any excess.

- In a small saucepan, heat the milk over medium heat until very hot but not boiling. Add the chocolate and stir constantly until melted. Whisk thoroughly to aerate it. Add the seltzer and stir.

- Divide the liquid and froth equally among the glasses. Gently add a melon ball–size scoop of ice cream to each glass. Slide 2 maraschino cherries each onto 4 heatproof swizzle sticks or skewers and stand one in each glass. Serve immediately.

st.nicholas'sreward

This über-rich cup of hot drinking chocolate is the perfect reward for those on St. Nicholas's "very good" list this year. Essentially a liquid chocolate bar for adults, this recipe achieves ultimate richness when you select bittersweet chocolate with 62 to 72 percent cacao. Serve in demitasse cups for a continental flair—and be prepared to make more when people beg for a second helping.

Serves 4

5 ounces bittersweet chocolate (62 to 72% cacao), coarsely chopped
¼ cup heavy cream
1 cup whole milk
1 teaspoon vanilla extract

- Put the chocolate and cream in a small saucepan over low heat. When the chocolate starts to melt, about 3 minutes, stir to blend. When the chocolate is completely melted and incorporated into the cream, add the milk and vanilla. Increase the heat to medium and stir often until the milk is warm, 3 to 4 minutes longer.

- Serve in demitasse cups or small mugs.

snowflakevanillawhitechocolate

White as snow but devilishly rich, this drink is a well-deserved comfort at the end of a long day. Serve it plain, or dress it up with marshmallows or a peppermint candy cane. It is essential to make this drink with genuine white chocolate made from cocoa butter, and not confectionery coating or a vegetable fat–based substitute. Because white chocolate consists mostly of cocoa butter, it melts very readily, so stir this mixture almost constantly to emulsify it and keep it from boiling over.

Serves 2

½ cup heavy cream
8 ounces white chocolate, coarsely chopped
1 teaspoon vanilla extract
1 cup plus 1 tablespoon whole milk
2 teaspoons cornstarch

- Combine the cream, white chocolate, vanilla extract, and the 1 cup milk in a small saucepan over medium heat. Bring to an active simmer to scald the milk, then lower the heat and simmer, stirring frequently, until the chocolate is melted and the mixture is heated through, about 5 minutes.

- In a small bowl, whisk the cornstarch into the 1 tablespoon milk, then add it to the saucepan, whisking constantly. Continue to simmer, whisking frequently, until slightly thickened and heated through, about 2 minutes longer.

- Serve hot in your finest china cups and saucers or fanciful mugs.

café singapore

The lure of exotic aromatic spices found in the outdoor markets of Singapore inspired this fragrant coffee. Star anise, known as *bunga lawang* in Malay, is a sweet and pungent star-shaped flower pod with a magical flavor. Green cardamom, which is equally at home in sweet and savory dishes, is also delicious in coffee. Serve without the whipped cream if you prefer a stronger flavor.

Serves 4

2 cups strong, freshly brewed coffee
2 whole star anise pods
2 green cardamom pods, cracked
2 teaspoons dark brown sugar
¼ cup whipping cream, lightly whipped with 1 teaspoon sugar
Pinch of ground cinnamon for garnish

- Combine the coffee, star anise, and cardamom in a small saucepan over medium-low heat, and warm for 5 minutes to infuse the coffee with the aromatic oils from the spices. Strain the coffee into a 4-cup glass measuring cup or small pitcher, add the sugar, and stir until dissolved.

- Fill each of four cups one-third full with whipped cream, then carefully pour the coffee into the middle of each cup, directly through the center of the cream, until full. Use a fine-mesh sieve to gently tap a light dusting of cinnamon over the cream.

mintchocolatecocktail

This variation on a classic European cocoa-making technique yields a dry and crisply refreshing hot drink. Combining chocolate and mint, this hot cocoa cocktail also includes cachaça, a sugarcane distillation best known as the key ingredient in Brazil's national drink, the caipirinha.

Serves 2

2 teaspoons Dutch process cocoa powder
2 teaspoons superfine sugar
2 teaspoons whipping cream
2 teaspoons cachaça
2 teaspoons 100-proof peppermint schnapps
1½ cups freshly boiled water

- Mix 1 teaspoon of the cocoa and 1 teaspoon of the sugar in each of two mugs. Add 1 teaspoon of the cream to each and stir until the sugar is completely dissolved and a smooth paste forms. Add 1 teaspoon of the cachaça and 1 teaspoon of the peppermint schnapps to each mug and stir well, then pour ¾ cup of the water into each and stir until thoroughly combined.

- Serve immediately.

caféflorentine

Inspired by the flavors of orange and almond in a traditional Florentine cookie, this sophisticated coffee drink combines Grand Marnier and amaretto for a delicious match. A cup of Café Florentine is divinely accented by a piece of dark bittersweet chocolate or chocolate-dipped Florentine cookies on the side.

Serves 4

¼ cup (2 ounces) Grand Marnier
2 tablespoons (1 ounce) amaretto
1 cup strong, freshly brewed coffee
1 generous tablespoon caramel or vanilla syrup
¼ cup light cream
4 pieces of bittersweet chocolate or 8 Florentine cookies for garnish

- Combine the liqueurs and coffee in a small saucepan over medium heat and bring to a low simmer. Stir in the syrup, lower the heat, and continue to cook at the lowest possible simmer until just heated through, 2 to 3 minutes. Remove from the heat, add the cream, and mix well.

- Serve in preheated demitasse cups with chocolate or cookies on the side.

chapter 2
teas, tonics, and tisanes

thebonfire

Red as fire and impressively flamboyant, the Bonfire is proudly nonalcoholic. But that doesn't mean this is a sappy drink. A healthy dose of black peppercorns and Peppadew Mild Piquanté Peppers imparts bite to this stunning beverage. Grown in South Africa, these chubby little peppers have an addictive flavor that makes them a perfect accompaniment to cocktails—as a garnish, an ingredient, or both.

Serves 6

2 10-ounce cans frozen strawberry daiquiri drink mix
4 cups water
2 tablespoons whole black peppercorns
1½ teaspoons whole allspice berries
10 Peppadew Mild Piquanté Peppers
6 slices of lemon for garnish
6 Peppadew Mild Piquanté Peppers for garnish

- Combine the frozen daiquiri mix and the water in a saucepan over medium heat and bring to a simmer. Stir to mix well, add the peppercorns, allspice, and the 10 peppers (plucked from the jar, not drained), lower the heat, and simmer gently for 15 minutes.

- While the Bonfire is heating through, prepare the garnishes. For each serving, bend a lemon slice and slide it onto a heatproof skewer, followed by a pepper.

- Strain the Bonfire into a pitcher, then pour it into tall heatproof glasses. Add the garnish and serve very hot.

whiteginger

White tea, which is light in flavor and refreshing, is the perfect base for this snappy drink. Brew white tea with cooler water than you would use to brew black tea and feel free to increase the amount of fresh ginger to taste.

Serves 4

8 tablespoons (8 grams) loose-leaf white tea or 6 white tea bags
1 teaspoon peeled and grated fresh ginger
¾ cup water, boiled and cooled to 170°F (about 4 minutes)
1 cup white grapefruit juice
1¼ cups white grape juice
1 tablespoon sugar

- Place the tea and ginger in a 1-quart prewarmed teapot (see note below) or 4-cup glass measuring cup and pour in the water. Stir, then cover and steep for 4 minutes.

- Strain the brewed tea into a small saucepan over medium heat, stir in the juices and sugar, and bring to a simmer. Lower the heat and simmer gently until just heated through, about 5 minutes.

- Serve in ceramic mugs or footed glass mugs.

Note: To keep your tea from cooling off too quickly and to avoid cracking your ceramic teapot, prewarm the teapot by filling it with hot (but not yet boiling) water from the kettle. Let the water sit for several minutes to warm the teapot, then drain it before steeping your tea.

orange, mango, and cinnamon tea

For optimum flavor, make this with Assam, Kenya, or Irish Breakfast, as these teas are full flavored enough to stand up to dilution with the orange juice. Mango puree, which has a rich, velvety texture, is a key ingredient here; look for it in Asian markets or specialty grocer's.

Serves 4

½ cup freshly squeezed orange juice, strained
1½ cups mango puree
1 5-inch Ceylon cinnamon stick, broken into 4 pieces
½ teaspoon lemon extract
1 tablespoon sugar
2 tablespoons (12 grams) loose-leaf black tea or 6 black tea bags
4 cups water, boiled and cooled to 195°F (about 1 minute)
4 lemon slices for garnish
4 orange slices for garnish
4 Ceylon cinnamon sticks for garnish

- Combine the juice, puree, cinnamon stick, lemon extract, and sugar in a saucepan over medium heat; bring to a simmer. Lower the heat and simmer gently until just heated through, about 5 minutes.

- Place the tea in a 1-quart prewarmed teapot (see note on facing page) and pour in the water. Stir, then cover and steep for 3 minutes.

- Strain the brewed tea into the saucepan and continue to heat at the lowest possible simmer for an additional 2 minutes.

- Place 1 slice each of lemon and orange and 1 cinnamon stick in each teacup and divide the hot tea evenly among the cups. Serve immediately.

spicymulledcider

When the air turns crisp and hillsides are ablaze in a glorious tapestry of color, it is officially autumn in New England, and apples are at their seasonal best. Mulled cider is practically synonymous with New England, where this hot beverage has been a specialty since colonial days. If you can, purchase freshly pressed cider from a local cider maker or apple orchard; otherwise, buy the darkest, cloudiest cider you can find at the grocer's.

Serves 4

3 cups sweet apple cider
4 whole star anise pods
½ teaspoon whole allspice berries
1 teaspoon whole cloves
1 5-inch Ceylon cinnamon stick
4 white cardamom pods, cracked
2 slices of orange, quartered
2 slices of lemon, quartered

- Combine all of the ingredients in a saucepan over medium heat and bring to a low simmer. Lower the heat and continue to simmer gently for 30 minutes. Ladle into four mugs and serve steaming hot.

moroccanminttea

This aromatic and refreshing tea requires Chinese gunpowder green tea, fist-fuls of fresh mint (dried mint won't do), and European-style sugar cubes. In Morocco, where tea is drunk like water, this tea is made in curvaceous silver teapots with long spouts. Professional tea vendors gracefully pour tea from heights of a foot or more into tiny, delicate, gilded tea glasses, then stand nearby, ready to refill as needed.

Serves 4

4 teaspoons (8 grams) loose-leaf gunpowder green tea or
   5 gunpowder green tea bags
6 European-style sugar cubes
1 cup tightly packed fresh mint
3 cups water, boiled and cooled to 185°F (about 2 minutes)
4 thin slices of lemon

- Place the tea, sugar cubes, and mint in a 1-quart prewarmed teapot (see note on page 24) or 4-cup glass measuring cup. The mint may need to be pressed down into the pot. Pour in the water, stir, then cover and steep for 2 to 3 minutes.

- Place a lemon slice in each of four heatproof glasses and strain the brewed tea into the glasses.

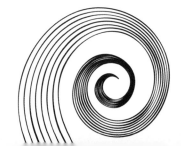

redrocket

Cinnamon oil—often used in combination with orange and clove oils—has been a prominent ingredient in spiced black tea blends since the 1920s. Cinnamon candies deliver a similar hot cinnamon flavor to this drink with no muss or fuss. For optimum flavor, use a smooth, full-bodied tea such as China Yunnan or Golden Nepal.

Serves 4

4 teaspoons (8 grams) loose-leaf black tea or 4 black tea bags
32 Red Hots cinnamon-flavored candies
4 5-inch Ceylon cinnamon sticks, each broken into 4 pieces
3 cups water, boiled and cooled to 195°F (about 1 minute)
2 slices of orange, halved, for garnish

- Place the tea, cinnamon candies, and cinnamon sticks in a 1-quart prewarmed teapot (see note on page 24) or 4-cup glass measuring cup and pour in the water. Stir, then cover and steep for 3 minutes.

- Put half of an orange slice in each of four cups or mugs. Strain the brewed tea into the cups, dividing it evenly among them.

masalachai

Throughout India, spiced black tea blends are consumed throughout the day by people of all ages. The mixture of spices varies depending on location, and many street corner chai wallahs (hot tea vendors) develop unique tea and spice combinations to woo potential customers. For the best flavor, use a finely cut Kenya or Assam black tea, or any brand of strong English or Irish black tea that you prefer. And even if you don't normally add milk or sugar to your tea, do so in this recipe to achieve the authentic flavor and color.

Serves 4

3 cups water
1½ cups whole milk
1 teaspoon whole cloves
¼ teaspoon freshly ground black pepper
3 5-inch Ceylon cinnamon sticks, each broken into 4 pieces
12 green cardamom pods, cracked
8 thin slices of fresh ginger
2 tablespoons (12 grams) loose-leaf black tea or 6 black tea bags
2 teaspoons Demerara sugar

• Combine the water and milk in a saucepan over medium heat, stir in the cloves, pepper, cinnamon sticks, cardamom, and ginger and bring to a simmer. Lower the heat and continue to simmer for 10 minutes. Add the tea and sugar, turn off the heat, and steep for 3 minutes.

• Stir once, strain into teacups or tea glasses, and serve hot.

monk'srobe

This richly colored drink, reminiscent of a chestnut-brown monk's robe, is a contemporary twist on a classic. In the 1960s, hot Dr Pepper was de rigueur on New Year's Day in many households. This updated version speaks to the increased sophistication of today's flavor seekers. Because Dr Pepper contains caffeine, this is a great pick-me-up on a cold winter afternoon.

Serves 4

3 cups Dr Pepper soda
1½ cups Ruby Red grapefruit juice
2 thick slices of fresh ginger
4 thin slices of lemon
4 thick slices of orange

- Combine the Dr Pepper, juice, and ginger in a saucepan over medium heat and bring to a low simmer. Don't boil the liquid, as this will make the soda flat.

- Place 1 slice each of lemon and orange in each of four mugs or cups and divide the hot beverage evenly among them. Serve immediately.

snow**falling**onpines

Dissolving *matcha* (Japanese green tea powder) in hot water yields a velvety dark green liquid reminiscent of the pines and moss in Japanese tea gardens. Tea made with *matcha* powder tastes pleasantly bitter, a flavor that's complemented here by the blanket of lightly sweetened whipped cream floating on top. If you serve this in glasses or drinking bowls, you can watch the cream slowly striating into the *matcha*—a lovely spectacle that inspired the name of this drink. To add a holiday touch, sprinkle a glimmer of red sanding sugar on top of the cream.

Serves 2

2 cups water, boiled and cooled to 170°F (about 4 minutes)
2 teaspoons matcha powder
¼ cup heavy cream, lightly whipped with 1 teaspoon sugar, for garnish
Red sanding sugar for garnish (optional)

- Strain the matcha through a fine-meshed sieve into 2 heatproof glasses or drinking bowls. Add 1 cup of the water to each and whisk until the matcha powder is dissolved.

- Cover the entire surface of the tea with the cream to temporarily hide the wonderfully green matcha. Top with a sprinkle of red sanding sugar, if you choose, and serve right away.

rosycheeks

This sleek and refreshing beverage contains no alcohol, but the characteristic zippiness of pink grapefruit juice and astringency of cranberry juice combine to give this drink the sophistication of a well-made cocktail. The pink color virtually blushes with a rosy glow, hence the name.

Serves 4

½ cup Ruby Red grapefruit juice
½ cup cranberry juice cocktail
½ cup guava juice
¼ cup freshly squeezed lime juice

• Combine the grapefruit juice, cranberry juice cocktail, and guava juice in a small saucepan over medium heat and bring to a simmer. Lower the heat and continue to simmer until just heated through, about 5 minutes.

• Add the lime juice, stir, and serve straight up in sherry or port glasses.

redbushtisane

This tisane derives its name from a literal translation of *rooibos*, the Afrikaans word for a reddish brown South African herb used to make a caffeine-free herbal tea. It combines wonderfully with other flavors and can be served either hot or iced.

Serves 4

4 teaspoons (8 grams) loose-leaf rooibos or 4 rooibos tea bags
3 cups boiling water
1 cup raspberries, fresh or frozen
4 lemon wedges

- Place the rooibos leaves in a 1-quart prewarmed teapot (see note on page 24) or 4-cup glass measuring cup and pour in the water. Stir, then cover and steep for 3 minutes.

- Strain the brewed tisane into a glass measuring cup. Put the raspberries into a heatproof blender container and pour in half of the tisane. Blend on low speed for 5 to 10 seconds only. Strain the liquid through a fine-mesh sieve back into the measuring cup containing the rest of the tisane. (The mixture will be foamy and will take a few minutes to drain through the sieve.) Press the raspberry pulp against the sieve with a spatula to release as much juice as possible.

- Transfer to a saucepan over medium heat and bring to a low simmer.

- Squeeze the juice of a lemon wedge into each of four cups and divide the tisane evenly among them.

chapter 3

merry-makingcocktails

trulyblue

This richly satisfying drink gets its name from a combination of blueberry juice, blue curaçao, and crème de cassis. Made from the dried peel of bitter oranges, blue curaçao is the color of the midnight sky or the open ocean. Cassis, made from currants, is used to make liqueur or syrup; either one can be used here. This drink tastes best when served as hot as possible, but be careful not to let it boil, as you don't want to burn off the alcohol. For best flavor and color, use wild blueberry juice, such as Wyman's. Then your drink will truly be blue.

Serves 4

2 cups wild blueberry juice
¼ cup (2 ounces) blue curaçao
¼ cup (2 ounces) crème de cassis or cassis syrup
¼ cup (2 ounces) Stoli Blueberi vodka
4 lemon twists for garnish (see page xi)

- Combine the juice, curaçao, crème de cassis, and vodka in a saucepan over medium heat and bring to a low simmer.

- Put a lemon twist in each of four demitasse cups and divide the warm drink evenly among the cups. Serve immediately.

hotwasabiredsnapper

In Paris in the 1920s, Fernand Petiot created a cocktail that he dubbed the Bloody Mary. Later, when he was head bartender at New York's stylish King Cole Bar in the St. Regis Hotel, Petiot spiced up the drink and renamed it the Red Snapper. Although the new name didn't stick, the new recipe did, and it will be forever known as the Bloody Mary.

This is yet another take on that famous cocktail. Not only is it served hot, it's also modernized once again, drawing inspiration from the bowl of Japanese snacks with wasabi peas that is served to patrons at the King Cole Bar.

Serves 4

2 tablespoons wasabi powder

2 tablespoons warm water

2 cups tomato juice cocktail

1 cup beef stock, or 2 beef bouillon cubes dissolved in 1 cup
   boiling water

2 teaspoons Worcestershire sauce

2 teaspoons soy sauce

1 teaspoon salt

4 thin slices of fresh ginger

4 lemon wedges, halved crosswise, for garnish

4 green onions, with root end intact and green end trimmed to
   3 inches total, for garnish

2 tablespoons freshly squeezed lemon juice

2 teaspoons Sherry Pepper Sauce

½ cup (4 ounces) vodka

- In a small bowl, combine the wasabi powder and warm water. Mix to form a smooth, thin paste, then cover and set aside.

- Combine the tomato juice cocktail, stock, Worcestershire sauce, soy sauce, salt, and ginger in a saucepan over medium heat and bring to a simmer. Lower the heat and simmer gently until just heated through, about 5 minutes.

- Meanwhile, assemble the garnishes. For each, slide half of a lemon wedge onto a heatproof skewer, rind side up. Spear the green onion at a whimsical angle just where the green meets the white, stacking it atop the lemon, then follow with another half of a lemon wedge.

- Remove the tomato juice mixture from the heat and press the ginger pieces against the side of the pan to extract the juice; discard the ginger. Add the reserved wasabi paste, lemon juice, pepper sauce, and vodka, and stir until thoroughly combined.

- Pour into tall mugs or heatproof glasses, add the garnish, and serve immediately.

thebullettrain

Beware: this sleek and stylish drink named for Japan's high-speed train combines three types of alcohol. One too many will go to your head—fast. Meyer lemons have an appealing fragrance and flavor that's a cross between a lemon and an orange. They also have very thin skin, so be careful when cutting strips of zest. If you can't find Meyer lemons, substitute a blend of equal parts fresh lemon juice and fresh, pulp-free orange juice. To achieve the best flavor, use Japanese green tea, which has a deep vegetal quality. Chinese green tea has a tendency to be grassy and thin. The fruity and fragrant flavors of sake made in the *junmai ginjo* style are ideal in this hot cocktail.

Serves 4

1 tablespoon (5 grams) sencha or other loose-leaf Japanese green tea, or 4 Japanese green tea bags

2 cups water, boiled and cooled to 170°F (about 4 minutes)

½ cup (4 ounces) junmai ginjo sake

3 tablespoons (1½ ounces) Midori

2 scant teaspoons Absolut Citron

4 Meyer lemon twists for garnish (see page xi)

• Place the tea in a 1-quart prewarmed teapot (see note on page 24) or 4-cup glass measuring cup and pour in the water. Stir, then cover and steep for 3 minutes.

► continued on page 48

- Strain the brewed tea into a saucepan, add the sake, Midori, and Absolut Citron, and place over medium heat. Bring to a very low simmer, then remove from the heat immediately.

- Serve in small cordial, sherry, or white wine glasses. Place a lemon twist in each glass and divide the hot libation evenly among the glasses. Stir and serve piping hot.

wiltedmimosa

Although this version of a mimosa forgoes the bubbly for white wine, its pale golden color is seductive enough to serve in champagne flutes. Equally appropriate for a winter brunch or an evening cocktail, this delicious version of the classic is a fine accompaniment for a toast on any occasion.

Serves 4

1 cup (8 ounces) dry white wine
½ cup freshly squeezed orange juice, strained
½ cup (4 ounces) 30-proof triple sec
2 thin orange slices, halved, for garnish

- Combine the wine and juice in a small saucepan over medium heat and bring to a gentle simmer, then remove from the heat. Let the mixture sit for 1 minute.

- Pour into four champagne flutes and top each with 2 tablespoons of the triple sec and a half of an orange slice.

Note: The first choice for this drink is 30-proof triple sec because the strength of the alcohol blends well with the wine and it has a nice orange flavor. If you have trouble finding 30-proof triple sec, you can substitute ¼ cup 80-proof triple sec, but the orange flavor will be less pronounced. Another possibility is to use ½ cup of 80-proof triple sec, but gently warm it in a small saucepan and then ignite it to burn off some of the alcohol. Make sure the flame is extinguished before adding the triple sec to the drinks.

mistletoeandholly

This festive drink features the colors of the Christmas season: red, white, and green. Replace the fresh cranberry garnish with an old-fashioned candy cane if you wish. Either way, a dusting of matte green *matcha* (Japanese green tea powder) adds an elegant finishing touch and an appealing visual counterpoint. It's important to use 100-proof peppermint schnapps, as the 40-proof version doesn't provide the desired balance of flavors.

Serves 4

12 fresh cranberries for garnish
1½ cups cranberry juice cocktail
¼ cup (2 ounces) white crème de cacao
¼ cup (2 ounces) 100-proof peppermint schnapps
¼ cup heavy cream, lightly whipped with 1 teaspoon sugar,
   for garnish
Pinch of matcha powder for garnish

- Spear 3 cranberries each onto 4 bamboo skewers or heatproof swizzle sticks.

- Pour the cranberry juice into a small saucepan over medium heat and bring to a simmer. Lower the heat, add the crème de cacao and peppermint schnapps, and stir to blend and release some of the alcohol. Continue to cook over low heat for exactly 1 minute.

- Divide the hot beverage evenly among four heatproof footed glasses, and place a small spoonful of whipped cream in each. Garnish with the cranberry skewers, and use a fine-mesh sieve to gently tap a light dusting of matcha over the whipped cream. Serve hot.

wintertwilight

Nightfall comes early during the winter months, affording us the opportunity to settle in by the fire and dream the evening away. Serving this sophisticated drink in glassware reveals its splendid jewel-tone color, which mirrors the deep hues of a drawn-out midwinter sunset.

Serves 2

1 cup pomegranate juice
1 tablespoon (½ ounce) Chambord
¼ cup (2 ounces) cognac
1 slice of lemon, halved, for garnish (optional)

- Put the pomegranate juice in a small saucepan over medium heat and bring to a low simmer. Lower the heat, add the Chambord and cognac, and simmer gently until just heated through, about 2 minutes.

- Put half a slice of lemon in each of two heatproof footed glasses, divide the potion equally, and enjoy.

pan-asian pear william

Pear William (*Poire William*) is a colorless eau-de-vie (a term that means "water of life"). Eaux-de-vie are strong and fiery spirits with a high alcohol content. Distilled from a single variety of fruit (in this case pears), they have remarkable flavors and aromas. Calvados is a tawny colored brandy distilled from bittersweet varieties of heirloom cider apples. Use a fine, small spirits glass to showcase the golden, nearly crystal clear elegance of this potion.

Serves 2

2 tablespoons (1 ounce) junmai ginjo sake
2 tablespoons (1 ounce) Pear William eau-de-vie
2 teaspoons Calvados
¼ cup boiling water

- Combine the sake, Pear William, Calvados, and water in a small saucepan over medium heat and bring to a simmer.

- Ladle into sherry glasses or small, clear glass cups and serve steaming hot.

fireandice

Although the pale blue color of this drink suggests the glacial ice of frozen landscapes, one sip reveals its fiery heart. The combination of flavors—piquant chile peppers, tropical fruits, and lemon—definitely has a south of the border flair. If making more than two drinks, combine the ingredients in a small saucepan, heat until steaming but not boiling, and pour into a glass pitcher to serve.

Serves 2

2 tablespoons (1 ounce) Absolut Peppar
2 tablespoons (1 ounce) Hpnotiq
¼ cup (2 ounces) limoncello

- Combine the spirits in a glass measuring cup and microwave for 40 seconds on full power.

- Serve in your fanciest cordial, sherry, or port glasses.

upside-down provençal panaché

In the south of France, Provençal bars and cafés serve a popular cold drink made from a combination of lemonade and beer. Called a *panaché*, this refreshing low-alcohol drink is also remarkably thirst-quenching when served hot. Surprisingly, the beer still foams up and makes a head after it's heated, so be careful when pouring it into cups or glasses. To make an authentic version of the original Provençal beverage, use pilsner or any other pale lager with a relatively high alcohol content (around 5 percent), such as Stella Artois, Kronenbourg 1664, Beck's, Pilsner Urquell, Carlsberg, or Labatt Blue. The lemonade can be effervescent or not (many European lemonades are slightly sparkling), and it should be moderately sweet to balance the citrus snap and alcohol bite.

Serves 4

4 cups pale lager
2 cups sweet lemonade

- Mix the beer and lemonade together in a saucepan over medium heat and bring to a simmer. Lower the heat and simmer gently until just heated through, about 5 minutes.

- Divide evenly among heatproof glass tumblers and serve warm.

chapter 4

welcomecupsand
partypunches

admiral'srumandbrandypunch

Pineapples are a traditional symbol of hospitality and welcome, making this the perfect cup with which to greet your guests upon arrival. Position a glass punch bowl front and center on your table and let the golden color of this delicious concoction draw people in. The sweetness of the juice provides a perfect counterpoint to the deep warming sensation of the alcohol. Don't be fooled by the quantity of fruit juice in this drink—this punch packs a wallop.

Serves 4

1 cup apricot puree
2 cups pineapple juice
½ cup white grapefruit juice
½ cup (4 ounces) light rum
¼ cup (2 ounces) brandy
4 lime wedges for garnish

- Combine the apricot puree and juices in a saucepan over medium heat and bring to a low simmer. Lower the heat and simmer gently for 2 minutes more, then add the rum and brandy.

- Serve in heatproof punch cups or glasses. Place a lime wedge in each cup, divide the punch evenly among the cups, and serve warm.

westindiespineapplecup

The blend of light and dark rums accentuates the natural sweetness and aroma of pineapple in this classic Caribbean combination. Blood orange bitters imparts snap and verve, and clear mint syrup adds freshness.

Serves 4

2 cups ginger ale
¾ cup pineapple juice
Juice of 1 orange
1 tablespoon (½ ounce) blood orange bitters
½ teaspoon clear mint syrup
1 whole small orange
24 whole cloves
½ cup (4 ounces) dark rum
½ cup (4 ounces) light rum
1 whole lime

- Combine the ginger ale, juices, bitters, and mint syrup in a saucepan over medium heat and bring to a simmer. Lower the heat and simmer gently until just heated through, about 5 minutes.

- Cut the orange lengthwise into 8 wedges. Stud the peel of each wedge with 3 cloves, then place 2 wedges in each of four heatproof punch cups.

- Stir the rums into the punch and continue to simmer until heated through, about 1 minute more.

- Cut the lime in half crosswise and squeeze about 1 teaspoon of juice over the orange sections in each cup. Divide the punch evenly among the cups and serve immediately.

glühwein

This popular European punch is made from whatever wine is readily available in local production. Because red wine can be too tannic and white wine too mild, this version uses both. Use hard cider for a stronger, drier brew. Forest honey is a strong, dark honey preferred by Europeans, but any dark honey will work here.

Serves 4

1½ cups (12 ounces) white wine
1½ cups (12 ounces) red wine
1½ cups (12 ounces) hard cider, or ¾ cup sweet apple cider
2 tablespoons (1 ounce) brandy (optional)
12 whole cloves
6 whole black peppercorns
1 hard cinnamon stick
3 orange twists (see page xi)
2 lemon twists (see page xi)
2 thick slices of orange
2 thin slices of lemon
1 scant tablespoon forest or other dark honey
Pinch of freshly grated nutmeg (optional)

- Combine the wines, cider, and brandy in a saucepan over the lowest possible heat. Stir in the cloves, peppercorns, and cinnamon stick and mull for 15 minutes. Add the citrus twists, citrus slices, and honey and continue mulling for 10 minutes more.

- Serve in pure white cups with saucers, garnished with the nutmeg.

wassail

Although the holiday wassail bowl is popularly associated with medieval England, it was also part of even earlier Norse and Saxon traditions of celebrating the passage out of the darkest nights of winter and into a new year. Today, wassail remains an essential component of revelries hosted on Twelfth Night (January 5), at the end of the Christmas season. If you want to make a larger wassail, this recipe can be scaled up easily by doubling the liquids, apples, and toast and increasing the spices by half.

Serves 4

3 Macintosh apples, cored
1 tablespoon salted butter, divided into 3 pats
4 cups (32 ounces) ale
1 cup (8 ounces) dry sherry
½ cup (4 ounces) white port
24 whole cloves
16 white cardamom pods, cracked
4 thin slices of fresh ginger
½ teaspoon ground ginger
½ teaspoon ground cinnamon
¼ cup dark brown sugar
4 5-inch Ceylon cinnamon sticks
6 small pieces of toast, crusts removed
Pinch of freshly grated nutmeg
4 Ceylon cinnamon sticks for garnish

► continued on page 66

- Preheat the oven to 325°F. Place the apples in a small roasting pan and add water to a depth of 1 inch. Place a pat of butter on each apple, then bake for 30 minutes, until tender but not mushy. Transfer the apples to a large heatproof punch bowl.

- Combine the ale, sherry, port, cloves, cardamom, fresh and ground ginger, ground cinnamon, brown sugar, and 4 cinnamon sticks in a saucepan over medium heat and bring to a simmer. Lower the heat and simmer gently for 30 minutes.

- Add the toast to the punch bowl, sprinkle the nutmeg over the toast, then carefully pour in the wassail.

- Serve in mugs, tankards, or heatproof punch cups with a cinnamon stick swizzle.

vincuit

Vin cuit literally means "cooked wine," a name given to this drink by winemakers in the south of France. *Vin cuit* is made from pressed grape juice cooked down to a concentrate, which is sweetened with seasonal fruit such as quince and a handful of nuts and allowed to ferment naturally in an underground cellar. This punch-style heated version incorporates aromatic sweet spices, a touch of Aleppo pepper (a mild chile pepper grown in northern Syria), and Passoã, an exotic liqueur featuring passion fruit and tropical citrus flavors. The deep rose hue of this combination of fruit and spice reflects the pleasant warming experience you have while sipping the drink.

Serves 6

1 bottle (750 ml) white table wine
¾ cup (6 ounces) Passoã
2 tablespoons (1 ounce) blood orange bitters
2 thick slices of fresh ginger
¼ teaspoon ground cinnamon
¼ teaspoon ground ginger
¼ teaspoon crushed Aleppo pepper
Juice of 1 orange
6 thin slices of lime for garnish

- Combine the wine, Passoã, bitters, spices, and orange juice in a saucepan over medium heat and bring to a simmer. Lower the heat and simmer gently until just heated through, about 5 minutes.

- Place a slice of lime in each of six heatproof punch cups or glasses, and divide the vin cuit evenly among the cups. Serve immediately.

swedishglögg

Aquavit is that little touch of something special that's crucial to glögg, Scandinavia's most popular hot drink. A colorless liquor blessed with a spirited caraway flavor, aquavit combines seamlessly with other spice flavors. In the cold, dark winter months, glögg is a favorite cocktail-hour beverage or predinner libation. In honor of Swedish tradition, serve with spiced almonds, *pepparkaka*, or gingersnaps.

Serves 6

1 bottle (750 ml) red wine
¾ cup (6 ounces) aquavit
¾ cup (6 ounces) Madeira
5 5-inch Ceylon cinnamon sticks
8 white cardamom pods, cracked
3 tablespoons diced candied orange peel
1 tablespoon sugar
2 tablespoons raisins
2 tablespoons blanched almonds, slivered or whole

- Combine the wine, aquavit, and Madeira in a saucepan over medium heat, stir in the cinnamon, cardamom, orange peel, and sugar and bring to a simmer. Lower the heat and simmer gently for 5 minutes, being careful not to let the glögg boil. Add the raisins and almonds and simmer 5 minutes longer.

- Discard the cinnamon, cardamom, and orange peel. Ladle the glögg into heatproof punch cups and serve with several raisins and almonds in each cup, if you choose.

ponchedefrutascaliente

Ponche de frutas is a humble, nonalcoholic punch, usually served cold, that originated in Mexico to celebrate the bounty of fresh, ripe fruit. The beauty of fresh fruit is that the various flavors harmonize wonderfully, no matter what the combination, so feel free to substitute depending on what's available in the market.

Serves 4

1 large apple, quartered and cored
2 oranges, quartered and center pith removed
1 lemon, quartered and center pith removed
1 lime, quartered and center pith removed
½ fresh pineapple, trimmed and cut into 8 chunks
2 cups sweet apple cider
2 cups white grape juice
1 cup sweet lemonade
Red and green grapes for garnish
¼ cup caramel, vanilla, or almond syrup for frosting the grapes
1 tablespoon superfine sugar for frosting the grapes

• Combine the apple, oranges, lemon, lime, pineapple, cider, grape juice, and lemonade in a large pot and bring to a boil over medium-high heat. Lower the heat and simmer gently for 30 minutes, stirring every 10 minutes to submerge the pieces of fruit; don't overcook the fruit.

• Meanwhile, destem the grapes, remove any seeds, and place them on a tray. Put the syrup into a small bowl, dip the tines of a fork into the syrup, and drizzle the syrup over the grapes in random patterns; don't cover the grapes completely with the syrup. Set the grapes aside for 10 to 15 minutes

► continued on page 72

to let the syrup dry and set up. Frost the grapes by dusting them lightly with the superfine sugar—the sugar will stick to the dried syrup. Spear several grapes each onto 4 bamboo skewers or heatproof swizzle sticks.

• Pour the ponche into an attractive heatproof pitcher and serve in heatproof glass mugs or tumblers at your preferred temperature, from piping hot to pleasantly warm. Garnish each serving with a swizzle stick of sugar-frosted grapes.

gingeredpearandapplepunch

Sweet apples and ripe pears—this perfect union of seasonal fruit flavors is beautifully complemented by the sophisticated snap of fresh ginger. A slice of fresh lemon floating in each cup adds a hint of tartness that flirts nicely with the ginger.

Serves 4

2 cups pear nectar
1½ cups sweet apple cider
2 teaspoons peeled and grated fresh ginger
¼ teaspoon freshly ground white pepper
4 slices of lemon for garnish

- Combine the pear nectar, cider, and ginger in a saucepan over medium heat and bring to the lowest possible simmer. Lower the heat, add the pepper, and continue to simmer gently for 2 minutes more.

- Place a lemon slice in each of four mugs or cups and divide the gingered punch equally among them. Serve very hot.

cranberryclaretcup

This jewel-tone red wine punch derives its distinguished flavor from brandy, tart cranberry juice, and a blend of sweet, warm spices. This is a real crowd-pleaser, so it's unlikely that you'll have any left over, but if you do, refrigerate it to use later as a delicious poaching liquid for pears or to make a hot fruit soup.

Serves 12 or more

1 bottle (750 ml) red Bordeaux wine
4 cups cranberry juice cocktail
1 cup (8 ounces) brandy
¼ cup sugar
12 whole allspice berries
8 whole cloves
8 thin slices of fresh ginger
2 5-inch Ceylon cinnamon sticks
2 teaspoons whole coriander seeds
1 lemon cut into 8 wedges

• Combine all of the ingredients in a large saucepan over medium heat and bring to a very low simmer. Lower the heat and simmer gently for 30 to 40 minutes, stirring occasionally.

• Ladle into heatproof punch cups or demitasse cups and serve warm.

angel'skiss

This drink turns a classic piña colada on its head. In addition to being served hot, the Angel's Kiss has more pineapple juice and uses frozen piña colada mix in place of heavily sweetened cream of coconut. The combination of rum and ginger brandy induces a pleasantly warm feeling. Some say it's like being kissed by an angel—a tropical angel, that is.

Serves 2

1 cup pineapple juice
1 cup frozen piña colada mix, thawed but not reconstituted
¼ cup (2 ounces) dark rum
¼ cup (2 ounces) ginger brandy
¼ cup heavy cream, firmly whipped with 1 teaspoon sugar, for garnish

• Combine the pineapple juice and piña colada mix in a small saucepan over medium heat and bring to a low simmer. Add the rum and ginger brandy, lower the heat, and continue to simmer gently for 2 minutes more.

• Serve in heatproof footed glass mugs, topped with a generous dollop of whipped cream.

chapter 5

winterwarmersand
sweetdreamers

hotbutteredrum

Although this classic toddy has been popular for generations, it's so delicious and easy to make that it will doubtless remain in demand for years to come. And when you're chilled to the bone, few hot libations can match the power of hot buttered rum to warm you from head to toe.

Serves 2

2 teaspoons light brown sugar
4 tablespoons (2 ounces) dark rum
1 slice of lemon, quartered
1½ cups boiling water
2 teaspoons salted butter

- Prepare the hot buttered rum in whatever you'll serve it in; ideally mugs, cups with saucers, or heatproof footed glass mugs. Place 1 teaspoon of the sugar and 2 tablespoons of the rum in each serving cup and stir until the sugar is completely dissolved. Add 2 quarters of the lemon slice and ¾ cup of boiling water to each cup. Top each with 1 teaspoon of butter and serve immediately.

hottoddy

Sometimes it's hard to improve on a classic, so this preparation of a perennial cold-weather favorite is very traditional. If you wish, you can improvise with cognac, rum, or whiskey, or even try adding black tea instead of hot water. But whatever you choose to use, don't forget the sugar and the lemon.

Serves 2

½ cup (4 ounces) brandy or cognac
2 teaspoons light brown sugar
2 lemon twists (see page xi)
1½ cups boiling water

• Put ¼ cup of the brandy in each of two mugs or cups. Add 1 teaspoon sugar and a lemon twist to each, then pour ¾ cup of the water into each.

• Stir briefly to melt the sugar and release the flavorful oils from the lemon, and enjoy.

dutchtreat

Anise and honey are commonly used to flavor Dutch sweets. Here we've combined them in a creamy quaff that features Pernod, a bracing French aniseed-based liqueur. For the best flavor, use honey with a floral bouquet, such as lavender, orange blossom, or wildflower honey. Whether you make a single recipe for an intimate group or a huge batch for a crowd, it's easy to prepare, and it makes a delicious accompaniment to gingersnaps, blondies, or carrot cake. Although this recipe calls for Pernod, you can substitute Ricard Anise, Pastis 51, or any generic anisette.

Serves 4

2 cups whole milk
1 tablespoon honey
3 tablespoons (1½ ounces) Pernod

- Scald the milk in a small saucepan over medium-high heat. The milk will be at the right temperature when tiny bubbles and a skin start to form all over the surface; this is critical to achieve the proper flavor in the finished drink. At this point, add the honey and whisk well. Stir in the Pernod and remove from the heat immediately.

- Divide evenly among four demitasse cups and serve right away.

athollbrose

Legend has it that this concoction allowed the Earl of Atholl to defeat his enemies during a Highland rebellion in 1475. He had the rebels well filled with this intoxicating beverage, after which they were easily overcome. The oatmeal broth ("brose") provides a creamy and luxurious base for tempering the fire of the Scotch whisky and Drambuie. The addition of Scottish heather honey keeps the flavors of this hot drink authentic.

Serves 2

1 cup uncooked oatmeal
1½ cups cold water
1 tablespoon Scottish heather honey or wildflower honey
¼ cup (2 ounces) Drambuie
2 tablespoons (1 ounce) Scotch whisky
¼ cup heavy cream, lightly whipped with 1 teaspoon sugar,
   for garnish

• Stir the oatmeal and water together in a small bowl. Cover and let sit for 1 hour, stirring gently every 15 to 20 minutes.

• Strain the oatmeal broth into a saucepan using a fine-mesh sieve. Press the oatmeal against the side of the sieve with a wooden spoon until almost dry to extract as much oatmeal broth as possible. Discard the solids, set the saucepan over medium heat, and bring to a low simmer. Lower the heat, stir in the honey, Drambuie, and Scotch, and simmer gently until just heated through, about 5 minutes.

• Serve in espresso-sized cups, topping each with a spoonful of whipped cream.

hotspeculatius

In Germany and Holland, the Christmas holidays wouldn't be complete without a selection of traditional spiced cookies. This hot drink was created in honor of *lebkuchen*, the popular German gingerbread cookie, and *speculatius*, Holland's thin, crisp windmill-shaped almond cookie. This wonderfully rich and creamy drink is the perfect messenger of holiday cheer.

Serves 2

2 cups whole milk
3½ ounces marzipan, chopped
1 tablespoon (½ ounce) amaretto
4 tablespoons (2 ounces) Bailey's Irish Cream
2 tablespoons (1 ounce) ginger brandy
Large pinch of ground cinnamon
Large pinch of ground cloves
Pinch of ground cardamom

• Combine the milk, marzipan, amaretto, Bailey's, and ginger brandy in a small saucepan over medium heat and bring to a simmer. Stir occaisonally to incorporate the marzipan. Lower the heat and simmer gently until just heated through, about 5 minutes. Stir in the cinnamon, cloves, and cardamom and simmer for another 2 minutes to release the aromatic oils from the spices.

• Strain into two large mugs and enjoy—with or without a namesake cookie.

tresleches

This nonalcoholic, eggless drink is a delicious alternative to traditional holiday eggnog. In Mexico, *tres leches* (which means "three milks") refers to a festive layer cake made with a combination of milk, cream, and sweetened condensed milk. Inspired by that distinctive flavor, this drink is further embellished with bananas, cinnamon, and orange juice. Ginger ale gives the drink its creamy, almost-thick-enough-to-stand-a-spoon-in texture. Be sure to open a fresh bottle of ginger ale for maximum carbonation, and don't be surprised when the mixture foams up as the ginger ale is added.

Serves 4

2 bananas, coarsely chopped
1 cup freshly squeezed orange juice, strained
½ teaspoon ground cinnamon
1 cup whole milk
1 cup light cream
1 14-ounce can sweetened condensed milk
1½ cups ginger ale

- Put the bananas, orange juice, and cinnamon in a blender and puree until smooth, about 40 seconds or a half dozen pulses.

- Combine the milk, cream, and condensed milk in a saucepan over medium heat, stir in the banana puree, and bring to a simmer. Lower the heat and simmer gently until just heated through, about 8 minutes. Add the ginger ale and stir continuously until heated through. Do not boil or the drink may curdle.

- Divide evenly among four Mexican-style pottery mugs and serve immediately.

highlandfling

Any good Scotsman would agree that the secret blend of herbs and spices in Drambuie lends this delicious liqueur a unique, complex flavor. For this libation, be sure to use fresh sage leaves and Meyer lemons. Fortunately, the season for this stellar citrus fruit is late fall and winter—perfect timing for use in hot drinks.

Serves 2

> 1 cup freshly squeezed orange juice, strained
> 10 fresh sage leaves, each approximately 1½ inches long
> ¼ cup freshly squeezed Meyer lemon juice, strained
> 6 tablespoons (3 ounces) Drambuie

- Combine the orange juice and sage leaves in a small saucepan over medium heat and bring to a simmer. Lower the heat and continue to simmer gently for 5 minutes, until the sage leaves have softened. Press the sage leaves against the side of the saucepan to extract all of their flavor, then discard the leaves (or reserve for garnish). Add the lemon juice and Drambuie and simmer for 1 minute more.

- Serve in heatproof glasses or footed glass mugs with a sage leaf garnish.

lamb'swool

Make no mistake, this innocent-sounding draught is no nursery sipper—it packs a punch. This cleverly named drink is adapted from an old English recipe designed to refresh weary travelers and warm them to their toes. To achieve the proper wool-like consistency, be sure to use regular applesauce, not apple butter or chunky, homestyle applesauce.

Serves 2

½ cup (4 ounces) cream sherry
½ cup (4 ounces) white port
2 5-inch Ceylon cinnamon sticks
6 whole cloves
3 lemon twists (see page xi)
¼ cup applesauce
Pinch of freshly grated nutmeg

- Combine the sherry, port, cinnamon, cloves, and lemon twists in a small saucepan over medium heat and bring to a simmer. Lower the heat and continue to cook at the lowest possible simmer until just heated through, about 2 minutes. Turn off the heat and let the libation sit for 30 minutes to allow the flavors to meld.

- Turn the heat to medium and bring just to a simmer. Strain into a heatproof measuring cup or small pitcher, then gently stir in the applesauce and nutmeg. Serve in sherry glasses or demitasse cups.

toastedcaramel

One sip is all you need to succumb to the charms of this sweet and creamy nightcap. Its understated color gives it an innocent appearance and it slides down your throat with satiny ease, but be warned: this seductive libation is deceptively potent. *Dulce de leche* is wonderfully thick and creamy in consistency. Scoop it right from the jar by the tablespoon and don't worry if you use more than is called for.

Serves 2

¼ cup dulce de leche
½ cup water
½ cup light cream
2 tablespoons (1 ounce) Frangelico
1 tablespoon (½ ounce) amaretto

• Combine the dulce de leche, water, and cream in a small saucepan over medium heat and bring to a simmer. Lower the heat and continue to cook at the lowest possible simmer until just heated through, about 2 minutes. Add the Frangelico and amaretto and mix well.

• Serve in teacups with saucers.

index